T0128398

Building
Self-esteem
through
Animal Stories

Animal Storybook No. 1

By Cathy Chargualaf

Animal Storybook No. 1

By Cathy Chargualaf

This belongs to:

Name:_____

Balboa Press books may be ordered through booksellers or by contacting:

Balboa Press
A Division of Hay House
1663 Liberty Drive
Bloomington, IN 47403
www.balboapress.com
1-(877) 407-4847

ISBN: 978-1-4525-7575-9 (sc)
ISBN: 978-1-4525-7576-6 (e)

Library of Congress Control Number: 2013911479

Printed in the United States of America.

Balboa Press rev. date: 04/23/2022

BALBOA.PRESS
A DIVISION OF HAY HOUSE

Dedicated to

*My grandchildren Isaiah, Aliyah, Mariah, Abbey,
Zoey, and Briella who fill my heart with joy.*

A special thanks to

*My husband Tom, without him you would not have this book in your
hands, he is my friend, supporter, and the love of my life,*

*My daughter Jasmine, my heart, whom I love so very much,
for being a light in this life,*

My parents for teaching me values that launch my desire to write this book,

*My talented brother Mike, professional illustrator, for providing
positive feedback on my story and illustrations,*

*My Aunt Carol for inspiring me to find the resources
to make this book possible,*

*My friends Joanne, Brenda, Cynthia and Patricia for encouraging
me to write and publish my work; Brandon for scanning my original
art work; Tom and Caroline for supporting and helping me proof my
work; Karl and David for being there to inspire my creativity.*

TABLE OF CONTENTS

Introduction for Parents xi

The little cat who cared 1
The little teddy bear that always helped others 7
The special little butterfly 11

INTRODUCTION FOR PARENTS

Please read first

Thank you for caring enough to give a child a gift that he or she will carry for the rest of their life.

We would love to hear from you how the Animal Storybook and affirmations changed or enhanced your child's self-esteem and self-worth.

Please send all testimonials to:
cathy.chargualaf@ca.rr.com

Instructions:

Sit down with your child. Give yourself enough time to follow through with each story, allowing time for your child's questions. Read each story. The order does not matter. If your child has a favorite animal start with that one first.
After reading a story, ask your child to recall when they helped someone. Have them remember a specific day and time. This will help your child remember what it felt like to help someone. Once your child has the event in mind, ask them to recall what was said, what was done, and how it felt. After your child has told his or her story, let them know how proud you are of them. Then have them recite, as an example, the same affirmation as the little cat, "I am caring."

Supporting your child in his or her own positive affirmation will build self-worth. Remember that praise builds good character and criticism cuts at the very heart of their self-esteem.

THE LITTLE CAT WHO CARED

Their once was a little cat that lived inside a house. One day, the little cat was taking a nap by the window.

She liked to curl up on the sofa cushion by the window and fall asleep. One afternoon, there was a loud bump. The little cat was scared and jumped off the cushion to see what had happened.

The little cat turned the corner in the living room and saw the family puppy on the floor. "What happened?", said the little cat.

"I was running and the rug slipped out from under me and I hit my ear on the chair.", said the sad puppy. "Oh, that must have hurt. I know how to make the pain go away fast." said the cat.

So, the little cat licked the puppy's ear and told him to think of something happy until it feels better.

The little cat snuggled up to the puppy and said, "You're going to be ok. I will stay here with you until you feel better. OK?".

The little cat smiled and said, "I have an idea, why don't we move the rug next to the window. That way you will not slip on it."

As the little puppy wiped the tears from his eyes, the little cat moved the rug next to the window where it makes her feel warm and cozy when taking a nap. The little cat jumped on her cushion by the window.

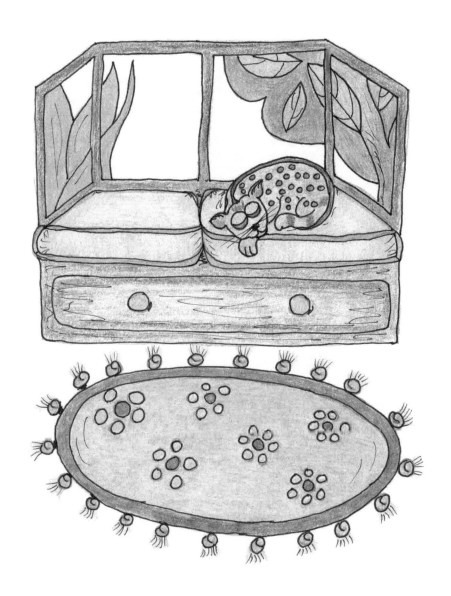

The mom cat saw what her little cat did and said, "I want you to know that what you did was nice and I am sure you made the little puppy feel better. You are a caring person, and now I want you to say, "I am caring."

The little cat said, "I am caring and that makes me happy.", with a big smile on her face.

THE LITTLE TEDDY BEAR THAT ALWAYS HELPED OTHERS

There once was a little teddy bear who lived with other bears. One day, as the little teddy bear was sitting on the bed, he noticed that all the other teddy bears were sad.

"Why are you all so sad?", said the little teddy bear.

"They forgot about us.", said one teddy bear. "We are lonely.", said the second teddy bear. "No one wants to play with us anymore.", said the third teddy bear.

The little teddy bear jumped off the bed and said, "I know what we can do! Follow me and don't worry. We are going to have some fun.", said the little teddy bear. The little teddy bear helped the other bears climb on the bed.

"OK. Now you have someone to play with... me!" said the little teddy bear. All the teddy bears played on the bed all day.

Later that night, the little teddy bear's mom said, "Sometimes, just being a friend can be a great help to someone in need. This is good, especially when someone is feeling sad. Look how you helped all the teddy bears find a friend today. I am so proud you."

"I want you to know that the little girl, who lives in this room, said she was so happy that she had so many wonderful teddy bears to play with.", said the mom teddy bear. "I want you to know that you made that little girl happy, too. You are a helpful person and now I want you to say, "I am helpful.""

The little teddy bear said, "I am helpful and that makes me happy.", with a big smile on her face.

THE SPECIAL LITTLE BUTTERFLY

Their once was a little caterpillar that lived in the woods. One day, the little caterpillar went for a walk. She stopped on the branch of a tree and began wondering what she would be when she grows up. She wondered, "Would I be like my mom?", "Would I be like my dad?". She wondered if she would be special just being herself.

From under the tree the little zebra said "Hey, why do you look so sad?".

"I want to be a beautiful butterfly when I grow up.", said the little caterpillar. "You can be. I will tell you how. Whatever you think you want to become, all you have to do is believe in yourself.", said the zebra.

"Keep a picture in your mind of how you will be a beautiful butterfly when you grow up. I will come back and we will see how you have changed.", said the little zebra.

The little zebra come back, much later, to the same tree and saw that the little caterpillar had become a cocoon.

The little caterpillar was sad because she was not a beautiful butterfly. Then she remembered what the little zebra had said to her, "All you have to do is believe." She thought to herself, "I believe I am a butterfly."

The little zebra went back to the same tree and saw how the caterpillar had changed from a cocoon, to a beautiful butterfly.

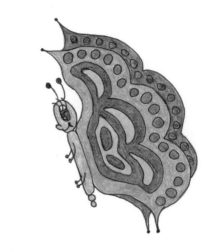

"Would you be my special friend?", said the little zebra. "Yes!", said the beautiful butterfly."

"I want you to know that you believed in yourself. There is something special in you little butterfly. You are special in many ways. Now I want you to say, "I am special.""

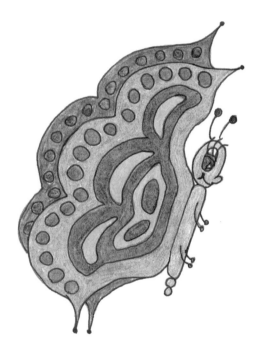

The beautiful butterfly said, "I am special and that makes me happy.", with a big smile on her face.

About the Author

Cathy Chargualaf is an author and founder of the Life Esteem Wellness Center. She provides positive impact coaching, seminars, and Life Esteem retreats.

Cathy teaches how to use powerful and effective tools to walk consciously and confidently through life's challenges from a centered and balanced place of possibility, opportunity, inner peace, abundance and joy. She helps adults and children increase their self-esteem and self-worth.

She offers a variety of services focused on bringing about physical and emotional well-being. Cathy and her husband, practice in Southern California. Website: www.cathychargualaf.com

Animal Storybooks:

Animal Storybook No. 1

Publisher: Balboa Press

By Cathy Chargualaf

Animal Storybook No. 2

Publisher: Balboa Press

By Cathy Chargualaf

Printed in the United States
by Baker & Taylor Publisher Services